Common Core
Standards Practice Workbook

Grade 5

Glenview, Illinois • Boston, Massachusetts
Chandler, Arizona • Upper Saddle River, New Jersey

ISBN-13: 978-0-328-75688-9
ISBN-10:   0-328-75688-1

4 5 6 7 8 9 10 V0N4 18 17 16 15 14 13

Grade 5 Contents

 **Standards Practice**

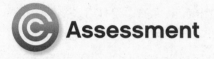 **Assessment**

About this Workbook

Pearson is pleased to offer this **Common Core Standards Practice Workbook**. In it, you will find pages to help you become good math thinkers and problem-solvers. It includes these pages:

- **Common Core Standards Practice pages.** For each Common Core Standard, you will find two pages of practice exercises. On these pages, you will find different kinds of exercises that are similar to the items expected to be on the end-of-year assessments you will be taking starting in 2014–2105. Some of the exercises will have more than one correct answer! Be sure to read each exercise carefully and be on the look-out for exercises that ask you to circle "all that apply" or "all that are correct." They will likely have more than one correct answer.

- **Practice for the Common Core Assessment.** You will find a practice assessment, similar to the Next Generation Assessment that you will be taking. The Practice End-of-Year Assessment has 45 items that are all aligned to the Common Core Standards for Mathematical Content. The two Performance Tasks focus on assessing the Standards for Mathematical Practice.

Name _____

Common Core Standards Practice

5.OA.A.1 Use parentheses, brackets, or braces in numerical expressions, and evaluate expressions with these symbols.

1. Which expression is equal to 2?

    A $24 \div (2 + 2) \times 5$

    B $(24 \div 2) + (2 \times 5)$

    C $(24 \div 2 + 2) \times 5$

    D $24 \div (2 + 2 \times 5)$

2. Tell whether the equation is true. Justify your answer.

$$2 + 1 \times 5 - 3 \overset{?}{=} (2 + 1) \times (5 - 3)$$

3. Evaluate the expression below.

    $(9 + 2) \times 6 - 5$

4. Evaluate the expression.

    $5 \div (4 - 3) \cdot 3$

5. Evaluate the expression.

    $20 \div (5 \times 2) + 3$

    A 5

    B 9

    C 11

    D 12

6. Which expression is equal to 7?

    A $(5 + 2) \times [6 - (3 + 2)]$

    B $5 + 2 \times 6 - (3 + 2)$

    C $(5 + 2) \times 6 - (3 + 2)$

    D $(5 + 2) \times [6 - (3 \times 2)]$

7. Kevin evaluated the expression below.

$75 - [6(8 - 6) + 3]$

- Step 1: $75 - [6 \cdot 2 + 3]$
- Step 2: $75 - [6 \cdot 5]$
- Step 3: $75 - 30$
- Step 4: 45

The teacher finds an error in Kevin's work.

a. Which step contains the error?

b. Explain the error.

8. Two students simplified the following expression.

Alexandra	**Joe**
$30 \div 2 - 4 \times 3 + 2$	$30 \div 2 - 4 \times 3 + 2$
$= 15 - 4 \times 3 + 2$	$= 15 - 4 \times 3 + 2$
$= 15 - 12 + 2$	$= 15 - 12 + 2$
$= 3 + 2$	$= 15 - 14$
$= 5$	$= 1$

a. Which student simplified the expression correctly?

b. What mistake was made?

Name _____

Common Core Standards Practice

5.OA.A.2 Write simple expressions that record calculations with numbers, and interpret numerical expressions without evaluating them.

1. Which expression matches this statement?

   Divide 24 by 6 less than 8.

   A $24 \div (8 - 6)$

   B $24 \div 8 - 6$

   C $(24 \div 6) - 8$

   D $[(24 \div 8) - 6]$

2. Each row in a box of chocolates contains 4 caramels and 8 creams. Which expression represents the number of chocolates in a box with 3 rows of chocolates?

   A $3 + (4 \times 8)$

   B $3 \times (4 + 8)$

   C $(3 \times 4) + (2 \times 8)$

   D $(4 \times 8) \times 3$

3. The price of an adult ticket to the museum is $6.00. The price of a student ticket is $4.00. Write an expression to represent the cost of 4 adult tickets and 8 student tickets.

4. Write an expression to match the statement below.

   Add 5 to 48 divided by 12.

5. Latisha and Raquel ordered two beverages for $1.50 each, two dinners for $12.99 each, and one dessert to share for $3.50. Which expression represents the cost of the meal for each person?

   A $1.50 + 2 \times 12.99 + 3.50 \div 2$
   B $(2 \times 1.50 + 2 \times 12.99 + 3.50) \div 2$
   C $2 \times (1.50 + 12.99 + 3.50)$
   D $(2 \times 1.50 + 12.99) + 3.50 \div 2$

6. Which expression matches the statement below?

   Find the product of 50 minus 5 and 4 divided by 2.

   A $(50 - 5) \times (4 \div 2)$
   B $50 - 5 \times 4 \div 2$
   C $50 \div 5 \times 4 \div 2$
   D $50 - 5 + 4 \div 2$

7. Write an expression to match the statement below.

   Divide the product of 4 and 5 by the sum of 2 and 8.

8. The table below shows the cost of several items sold at The Clothes Shack.

The Clothes Shack	
Item	Price per article ($)
Jeans	30
T-Shirt	15
Sweatshirt	20
Caps	10

Jason went to the Clothes Shack with $150. Write an expression to represent the amount of money Jason has remaining after buying 2 pairs of jeans, 3 T-shirts, and 2 sweatshirts.

Name _____

Common Core Standards Practice

5.OA.B.3 Generate two numerical patterns using two given rules. Identify apparent relationships between corresponding terms. Form ordered pairs consisting of corresponding terms from the two patterns, and graph the ordered pairs on a coordinate plane.

1. **a.** Generate two numerical sequences using the rules shown below.

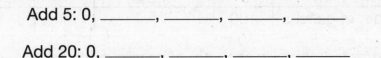

Add 5: 0, _____, _____, _____, _____

Add 20: 0, _____, _____, _____, _____

b. What relationship can you find between the second term in first sequence and the second term in the second sequence?

c. Does this relationship hold for all corresponding terms in the two sequences? Tell how you know.

2. Complete the following table.

Add 8.	8	16			
Subtract 2.	2	4			

3. Ama is emptying a large container of water. The container has 100 gallons of water. Ama opens the valve so that 5 gallons of water flow out each minute.

   a. Complete a table to show how much water flows out of the container over time.

Minutes	0						
Number of gallons	100						

   b. Write ordered pairs for each set of values in the table.

   c. Plot the ordered pairs on the coordinate grid.

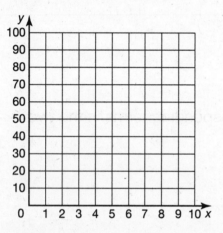

4. a. Write four ordered pairs by applying the rules "subtract 1 from the x-coordinate" and "add 2 to the y-coordinate." Begin at (5,0).

   Ordered Pairs: (5, 0), (_____, _____), (_____, _____), (_____, _____), (_____, _____)

   b. Graph the ordered pairs on the grid.

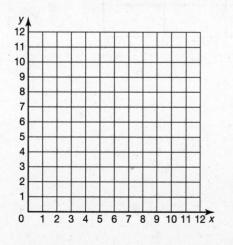

CC 6

Name _____

Common Core Standards Practice

5.NBT.A.1 Recognize that in a multi-digit number, a digit in one place represents 10 times as much as it represents in the place to its right and $\frac{1}{10}$ of what it represents in the place to its left.

1. How much greater is 500 than 5?

    A 5 times greater

    B 10 times greater

    C 100 times greater

    D 1000 times greater

2. Which describes the relationship between 20,000 and 200,000?

    A 20,000 is 10 times as much as 200,000.

    B 200,000 is $\frac{1}{10}$ of 20,000.

    C 20,000 is $\frac{1}{100}$ of 200,000.

    D 20,000 is $\frac{1}{10}$ of 200,000.

3. How is the value of 2 in the number 542 different from the value of 2 in the number 324?

4. How is the value of 4 in 864 related to the value of 4 in 846?

CC 7

5. How much greater is 300 than 3?

    A 10 times

    B 100 times

    C 1,000 times

    D 10,000 times

6. What is the relationship between 5,000 and 500,000?

    A 5,000 is $\frac{1}{10}$ the value of 500,000.

    B 5,000 is $\frac{1}{100}$ the value of 500,000.

    C 5,000 is 100 times the value of 500,000.

    D 5,000 is 10 times the value of 500,000.

7. What is the difference in place value between the 2 in 324 and the 2 in 0.324?

8. The total number of people who visited the Ocean Adventure Park last year was 7,040,836. What is the value of the digit 4 in this number?

9. How many tenths are in 13.58?

10. How many hundredths are in 401.308?

Name _____

Common Core Standards Practice

5.NBT.A.2 Explain patterns in the number of zeros of the product when multiplying a number by powers of 10, and explain patterns in the placement of the decimal point when a decimal is multiplied or divided by a power of 10. Use whole-number exponents to denote powers of 10.

1. Circle all of the expressions that equal 372,000.

372×10^3 $\qquad$ 3.72×10^6 $\qquad$ 372×10^4

37.2×10^4 $\qquad$ 37.2×10^3 $\qquad$ 3.72×10^5

2. Complete the table.

Expression	Product
5×10^1	50
5×10^2	
5×10^3	
5×10^4	

What pattern do you observe in the table?

3. Complete the table.

Expression	Quotient
$76 \div 10^1$	7.6
$76 \div 10^2$	
$76 \div 10^3$	
$76 \div 10^4$	

What pattern do you observe in the table?

CC 9

4. Draw a model to show the value of this expression.

$5 \div 10^2$

5. Match the numbers on the left with an equivalent expression on the right. Some may have more than one equivalent expression. Some may have no equivalent expressions.

0.67

$1067 \div 10^2$

$4.239 \div 10^3$

10.67

$67 \div 10^3$

1.067×10^1

4,239

$67 \div 10^2$

4.239×10^3

6. Circle all of the expressions that are equivalent to 1,795,000.

$1,795 \times 10^3$ 17.95×10^5 1.795×10^7

179.5×10^5 17.95×10^6 $1,795 \times 10^3$

Name _____

Common Core Standards Practice

5.NBT.A.3a Read, write, and compare decimals to thousandths. Read and write decimals to thousandths using base-ten numerals, number names, and expanded form.

1. Sharon is writing 4.072 in expanded form. What number makes the equation true?

   4.072 = 4 + 0.0 + _____ + 0.002

   A 7
   B 0.7
   C 0.07
   D 0.007

2. What is the standard form of the number below?

   10 + 1 + 0.9 + 0.02 + 0.003

   A 1192.3
   B 119.23
   C 1.1923
   D 11.923

3. Jeremy has a batting average of 0.235. What is the batting average written in expanded form?

4. Match these numbers with their expanded forms.

   3.6

   $4 \times 10 + 1 \times \frac{1}{10} + 5 \times \frac{1}{100}$

   3.06

   $3 \times 1 + 6 \times \frac{1}{100}$

   40.15

   $3 \times 1 + 6 \times \frac{1}{10}$

   4,015

   $4 \times 1000 + 1 \times 10 + 5 \times 1$

CC 11

5. Which show different forms of 5.39? Circle all that are equal to 5.39.

    A Five and thirty-nine hundredths

    B $539 \div 10^2$

    C $5 + 0.3 + 0.09$

    D 5 and 39 tenths

    E 0.539×10^2

    F 0.539×10^1

6. What is the expanded form of five and six hundred fourteen thousandths?

    A $5 + 0.6 + 0.01 + 0.004$

    B $5 + 0.06 + 0.01 + 0.004$

    C $5 + 0.06 + 0.001 + 0.004$

    D $5 + 0.6 + 0.001 + 0.0004$

7. Write these expressions in standard form.

    a. $(4 \times 1) + \left(6 \times \frac{1}{10}\right)$

    b. $4 \times 10 + 3 \times \frac{1}{10} + 7 \times \frac{1}{100} + 5 \times \frac{1}{1000}$

    c. $(9 \times 10) + \left(5 \times \frac{1}{10}\right)$

    d. $(9 \times 1) + \left(5 \times \frac{1}{100}\right)$

Name _____

Common Core Standards Practice

5.NBT.A.3b Read, write, and compare decimals to thousandths. Compare two decimals to thousandths based on meanings of the digits in each place, using >, =, and < symbols to record the results of comparisons.

1. Which of the following numbers is greater than 7.03?

   A 7.031

   B 7.030

   C 7.003

   D 7.0

   Explain how you know.

2. Which of the following lists three decimals between 8.6 and 9.2?

   A eight and seven tenths, 8.61, 8.5

   B eight and seven hundredths, 9.1, 9.0

   C eight and eight tenths, 9.21, 9.01

   D eight and seventy-five hundredths, 8.80, 9.19

3. The length of New York's subway is 368 km, while the length of Moscow's subway is 306.2 km. Which subway system is longer? Use >, <, or = to compare the two lengths. Then justify your answer using place value.

4. In each box, write <, >, or = to make a true sentence:

   a. 46.491 ☐ 46.577   **b.** 2.15 ☐ 2.150   **c.** 11.341 ☐ 11.34

   d. 0.495 ☐ 0.503   **e.** 0.080 ☐ 0.08   **f.** 8.70 ☐ 8.697

5. Matt completed his first race in 15.163 seconds. The time of his second race was 15.24 seconds. Which of the following shows the correct relationship between 15.163 and 15.24?

   A $15.163 < 15.24$

   B $15.163 > 15.24$

   C $15.24 < 15.163$

   D $15.24 = 15.163$

Justify your answer.

6. Which of the following numbers is less than 23.90?

   A 23.9

   B 23.09

   C 23.91

   D 23.92

7. Mrs Sanders bought 2 pumpkins. The first one weighed 4.89 kilograms; the second one weighed 4.9 kilograms. Use $>$, $<$, or $=$ to compare the weights.

Justify your answer.

8. Wendy, Todd, and Theresa went on a hike. They hiked 7.25 miles, 7.5 miles, and 7.245 miles. Order the distances from least to greatest.

Justify your answer using place value.

Name _____

Common Core Standards Practice

5.NBT.A.4 Use place value understanding to round decimals to any place.

1. What is 5.385 rounded to the nearest tenth?

   A 5.3

   B 5.4

   C 5.5

   D 5.6

2. What is 4.62 rounded to the nearest whole number?

   A 5

   B 4.5

   C 4.7

   D 4.5

3. Round these numbers to the nearest tenth.

   a. 182.886   d. 7.96

   b. 0.459   e. 0.3

   c. 4.06   f. 3.21

4. Round these numbers to the nearest hundredth.

   a. 182.886   d. 8.31

   b. 0.459   e. 8.072

   c. 0.172   f. 130.039

5. Which of these numbers, when rounded to the nearest hundredth, is 0.05? Circle all that round to 0.05.

0.049   0.057   0.052   0.44   0.55

6. What is 45.0189 rounded to the nearest thousandth?

A 45.018

B 45.0188

C 45.019

D 45.0289

7. What is 4.106 rounded to the nearest hundredth?

A 4.10

B 4.11

C 4.12

D 4.107

8. A box of uncooked spaghetti costs $0.1369 per ounce. How much is this cost to the nearest cent?

9. Roberto's baseball batting average is 0.278. What is his batting average rounded to the nearest hundredth?

10. Which of these numbers, when rounded to the nearest tenth, is 8.3? Circle all that round to 8.3.

8.28   8.24   8.33   8.36   8.25

Name _____

Common Core Standards Practice

5.NBT.B.5 Fluently multiply multi-digit whole numbers using the standard algorithm.

Find these products.

1. 42
   × 27

2. 632
   × 49

3. 38
   × 87

4. 155
   × 23

5. 76
   × 17

6. 41
   × 86

7. 138
   × 57

8. 209
   × 54

Find these products.

9. 19
    × 87

10. 397
    × 53

11. 441
    × 63

12. 445
    × 273

13. 632
    × 56

14. 518
    × 107

15. 479
    × 328

16. 169
    × 304

CC 18

Name _____

Common Core Standards Practice

5.NBT.B.6 Find whole-number quotients of whole numbers with up to four-digit dividends and two-digit divisors, using strategies based on place value, the properties of operations, and/or the relationship between multiplication and division. Illustrate and explain the calculation by using equations, rectangular arrays, and/or area models.

Solve these division problems.

1. $97\overline{)2,134}$

2. $69\overline{)2,898}$

3. A theater has 182 seats that are divided evenly into 14 rows. How many seats are in each row?

   a. Draw a model of the problem and write an equation that describes the model.

   b. Solve the equation you wrote.

4. Neil has 1,216 sports cards that he divides into 32 packages, each with the same number of cards. How many cards are in each package?

   a. Draw a model that represents this probem, and write an equation to match the model.

   b. Solve the equation you wrote.

Solve these division problems.

5. $68\overline{)1{,}904}$

6. $57\overline{)5{,}415}$

7. Marcia has 1,792 flowers for making centerpieces. Each centerpiece will have 64 flowers. How many centerpieces can she make?

   a. Draw a simple model that explains this probem, and write an equation that describes the model.

   b. Solve the equation you wrote.

8. A plant nursery will plant 1,560 trees in ten different plots of land. Each plot of land will have the same number of trees, planted in rows of 12.

   a. How many trees will be planted in each plot of land?

   b. How many rows of trees will be on each plot of land?

   c. Justify your solutions using equations or models.

Name _____

Common Core Standards Practice

5.NBT.B.7 Add, subtract, multiply, and divide decimals to hundredths, using concrete models or drawings and strategies based on place value, properties of operations, and/or the relationship between addition and subtraction; relate the strategy to a written method and explain the reasoning used.

1. The temperature increased from 58.7°F to 92.6°F. Find the difference between the two temperatures in degrees Fahrenheit.

2. The table shows the mass of four packages. What is the total mass of the packages?

Package	Mass (kg)
1	3.94
2	14.81
3	11.27
4	7.65

3. Alexandra went to the mall on Saturday and bought the items listed in the table. She bought each item at the discount price.

Item	Original Price ($)	Discount Price ($)
Bracelet	25.75	19.50
Hat	19.25	15.00

   a. What is the total cost of the items at their original prices?

   b. How much did Alexandra save?

   c. Explain how you determined how much she saved.

4. A car gets 28.45 miles on 1 gallon of gasoline. The gasoline tank holds 11.5 gallons.

   a. Describe how to find how far the driver can drive the car on a full tank of gasoline.

   b. How far can the driver go in this car on a full tank?

5. Three stores sell Cactus Cola. The stores sell the same bottles, but they group them in packs of either 6, 12, or 24 bottles.

Store A	6-pack	$3.45
Store B	12-pack	$5.25
Store C	24-pack	$10.99

   a. How can you tell which store sells a bottle of cola for the lowest price?

   b. Which store sells Cactus cola bottles for the lowest price? What is this price?

6. The table shows the admission price to a zoo.

Adult	$7.45
Student	$4.50
Child under 5	$3.75

The Chung family buys 2 adult tickets, 2 student tickets, and 1 child's ticket. What is the total cost of the tickets?

Name _____

Common Core Standards Practice

5.NF.A.1 Add and subtract fractions with unlike denominators (including mixed numbers) by replacing given fractions with equivalent fractions in such a way as to produce an equivalent sum or difference of fractions with like denominators.

1. Which of these is equal to the sum of $\frac{4}{6}$ and $\frac{4}{9}$? Circle all that are equal to the sum.

   $\frac{10}{9}$ $\frac{8}{15}$ $\frac{40}{36}$ $\frac{4}{15}$ $\frac{11}{7}$ $1\frac{2}{18}$

2. Which of these is equal to the difference of $\frac{8}{9}$ and $\frac{2}{3}$? Circle all that are equal to the difference.

   $\frac{1}{12}$ $\frac{2}{9}$ $\frac{9}{14}$ $\frac{1}{9}$ $\frac{4}{18}$ $1\frac{5}{9}$

3. Which equivalent fractions can you use to find the sum of $\frac{2}{8} + \frac{3}{9}$?

4. Find the sum.

   $\frac{2}{8} + \frac{3}{9}$

5. Which equivalent fractions can you use to find the difference of $5\frac{3}{12}$ and $1\frac{4}{9}$?

6. Find the difference.

   $5\frac{3}{12} - 1\frac{4}{9}$

7. Place these expressions in the appropriate column.

Less than 1	Equal to 1	Greater than 1

$\frac{1}{5} + \frac{3}{12}$ $\qquad$ $3\frac{1}{4} - 2\frac{1}{2}$ $\qquad$ $\frac{7}{12} + \frac{2}{3}$ $\qquad$ $3\frac{1}{3} - 1\frac{5}{6}$

$1\frac{1}{4} - \frac{9}{12}$ $\qquad$ $\frac{3}{12} + \frac{3}{4}$ $\qquad$ $1\frac{4}{18} - \frac{2}{9}$ $\qquad$ $\frac{1}{2} + \frac{5}{8}$

8. Which equivalent fractions can you use to find the sum of $2\frac{5}{6} + 1\frac{3}{4}$?

9. Find the sum.

$2\frac{5}{6} + 1\frac{3}{4}$

10. Which equivalent fractions can you use to find the difference of $2\frac{5}{6}$ and $\frac{9}{5}$?

11. Find the difference.

$2\frac{5}{6} - \frac{9}{5}$

Name _____

Common Core Standards Practice

5.NF.A.2 Solve word problems involving addition and subtraction of fractions referring to the same whole, including cases of unlike denominators, e.g., by using visual fraction models or equations to represent the problem. Use benchmark fractions and number sense of fractions to estimate mentally and assess the reasonableness of answers.

1. Alex practices his guitar $\frac{5}{8}$ of an hour on Wednesday and $3\frac{3}{4}$ hours on Thursday.

   a. Write an equation that can be used to determine how many hours Alex practiced his guitar on Wednesday and Thursday.

   b. Solve the equation you wrote.

2. Anna used $\frac{2}{5}$ yard of ribbon for one craft project and $\frac{3}{4}$ yard of ribbon for a second craft project.

   a. Estimate how much ribbon Anna used for the two projects.

   b. Use the number line to model the problem situation.

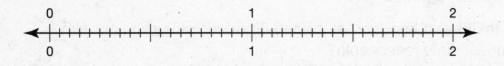

   c. How much ribbon did Anna use for the two craft projects?

3. Maria bought $1\frac{1}{2}$ pounds of nails for a carpentry project. She ended up with $\frac{3}{8}$ pound of nails when she finished the project.

    a. Write an equation that can be used to determine how much of the $1\frac{1}{2}$ pounds of nails Maria used.

    b. Solve the equation you wrote.

4. Jack ran $\frac{2}{8}$ mile and Roy ran $\frac{2}{3}$ mile.

    a. What benchmark fractions can be used to estimate how much farther Roy ran than Jack?

    b. Using the benchmark fractions, what is a reasonable estimate for the difference between the two distances?

    c. What is the actual difference?

5. Eva's new dog weighed $5\frac{7}{8}$ pounds when she first got him 4 weeks ago. Now he weighs $12\frac{1}{4}$ pounds.

    a. Eva thinks that her dog has gained 6 pounds since she got him. Is her estimate reasonable?

    b. How much weight has Eva's dog actually gained?

CC 26

Name _____

Common Core Standards Practice

5.NF.B.3 Interpret a fraction as division of the numerator by the denominator ($\frac{a}{b} = a \div b$). Solve word problems involving division of whole numbers leading to answers in the form of fractions or mixed numbers, e.g., by using visual fraction models or equations to represent the problem.

1. Which division expression matches the model?

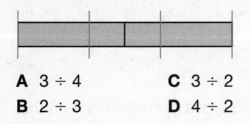

A $3 \div 4$ C $3 \div 2$

B $2 \div 3$ D $4 \div 2$

2. Which model matches the division expression?

$6 \div 4$

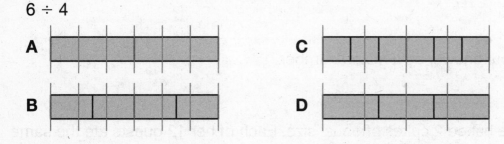

3. a. Use the bar model below to show 8 bars divided evenly into 5 parts.

b. Is each part bigger or smaller than the individual bars? Explain how you know.

4. a. Use the bar model below to show 5 bars divided evenly into 8 parts.

b. Is each part bigger or smaller than the individual bars? Explain how you know.

5. Eva has 35 apples. She divides them equally into 7 bags. Which fraction represents the number of apples Eva puts in each bag?

A $\frac{35}{7}$

B $\frac{7}{35}$

C $\frac{35}{5}$

D $\frac{28}{35}$

6. Beth has 8 acres of land. She wants to grow 5 types of crops, each on the same size plot.

  a. Write a division statement to represent the number of acres of land for each crop.

  b. Write your answer as a mixed number.

7. Ms. George baked 2 cakes of equal size. Each of her 12 guests ate the same amount of cake, and no cake was left over.

  a. What fraction of a cake did each guest eat?

  b. How do you think Ms. George cut the cakes into equal pieces? Explain.

8. Allen bought a 15-pound bag of ice. He distributed the ice evenly among 4 coolers. How many pounds of ice went into each cooler? Express your answer as a mixed number.

Name _____

Common Core Standards Practice

5.NF.B.4a Apply and extend previous understandings of multiplication to multiply a fraction or whole number by a fraction. Interpret the product $(\frac{a}{b}) \times q$ as a parts of a partition of q into b equal parts; equivalently, as the result of a sequence of operations $a \times q \div b$.

1. A baker uses $\frac{2}{3}$ of a stick of butter to make one batch of cookies. How many sticks of butter does she need to make 3 batches of cookies?

    a. The model below represents the problem situation. Explain the model.

    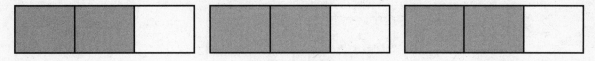

    b. What does each shaded part represent?

    c. How many shaded parts are in the model?

    d. Write an expression that can be used to determine how many sticks of butter the baker needs.

    e. How much butter does the baker need for three batches of cookies?

2. Use the model below to show $\frac{2}{5} \times 4$.

3. Explain why $2 \times \frac{3}{8}$ is equivalent to $2 \times 3 \times \frac{1}{8}$.

4. Match the model with the expression.

$\frac{2}{9} \times 3$

$4 \times \frac{1}{3}$

$\frac{3}{4} \times 2$

$5 \times \frac{1}{2}$

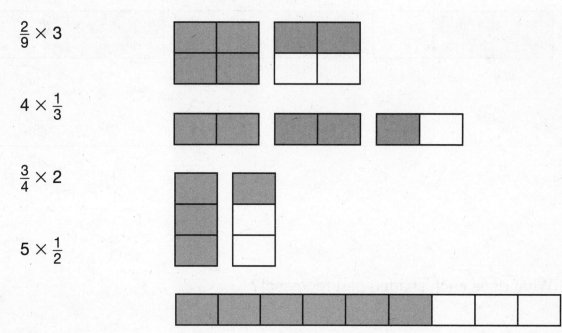

5. Draw a model to show $\frac{1}{4} \times \frac{2}{3}$. Then find the product.

6. Draw a model to show $5 \times \frac{4}{5}$. Then find the product.

Name _____

Common Core Standards Practice

5.NF.B.4b Apply and extend previous understandings of multiplication to multiply a fraction or whole number by a fraction. Find the area of a rectangle with fractional side lengths by tiling it with unit squares of the appropriate unit fraction side lengths, and show that the area is the same as would be found by multiplying the side lengths. Multiply fractional side lengths to find areas of rectangles, and represent fraction products as rectangular areas.

For 1–4, write an equation to find the area of the shaded rectangles. Then solve the equation.

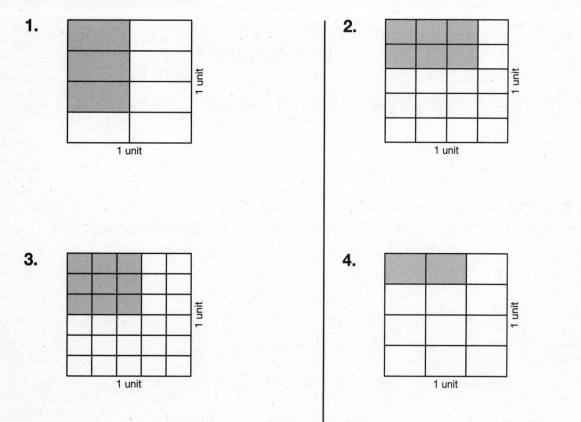

1.

2.

3.

4.

5. Angie got a new area rug for her room. The figure on the right shows the dimensions of her room and the area rug.

   a. What are the dimensions of the area rug?

   Width: _____

   Length: _____

   b. What is the area of the area rug?

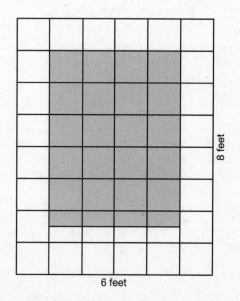

8 feet

6 feet

6. What is the area of a rectangle with length 5 feet and width $6\frac{1}{2}$ feet?

   A 30 ft²

   B $30\frac{1}{2}$ ft²

   C $34\frac{1}{2}$ ft²

   D $32\frac{1}{2}$ ft²

7. What is the area of a rectangle that is $8\frac{2}{5}$ inches long and 6 inches wide?

   A $5\frac{2}{5}$ in.²

   B $48\frac{2}{5}$ in.²

   C $50\frac{2}{5}$ in.²

   D $100\frac{4}{5}$ in.²

8. Find the area of a rectangle that is $6\frac{1}{3}$ inches long and $4\frac{3}{4}$ inches wide.

9. Jay arranges 18 feet of fencing into a rectangle that is 5 feet long and 4 feet wide. Show that he could make a larger area by arranging the fencing into a square.

10. John has a rectangular patio that is $6\frac{3}{4}$ yards long and $4\frac{1}{3}$ yards wide. What is the area of the patio?

Name _____

Common Core Standards Practice

5.NF.B.5a Interpret multiplication as scaling (resizing) by: Comparing the size of a product to the size of one factor on the basis of the size of the other factor, without performing the indicated multiplication.

1. Write the expressions in the appropriate place. You should NOT find the products of the expressions.

Less than 5	Equal to 5	Greater than 5

$5 \times \frac{3}{2}$ $\quad$ $5 \times \frac{2}{3}$ $\qquad$ $5 \times \frac{4}{3}$ $\qquad$ $\frac{1}{2} \times 10$

$\frac{1}{2} \times 5$ $\qquad$ $\frac{3}{3} \times 5$ $\qquad$ $\frac{7}{8} \times 5$ $\qquad$ $5 \times \frac{4}{4}$

2. For each statement 2a through 2d, circle YES if the statement is true or NO if the statement is not true.

   a. $\frac{3}{5} \times 5 > 5$ $\qquad$ YES $\qquad$ NO

   b. $\frac{3}{5} \times 5 > \frac{3}{5}$ $\qquad$ YES $\qquad$ NO

   c. $6 \times \frac{3}{2} > 6$ $\qquad$ YES $\qquad$ NO

   d. $6 \times \frac{3}{2} < \frac{3}{2}$ $\qquad$ YES $\qquad$ NO

3. Jeff feeds the family dog on Wednesdays and his sister Melody feeds the dog on Fridays. On Wednesday, Jeff gave the dog $\frac{5}{8}$ of an 8-ounce can of dog food. On Friday, Melody, gave the dog $\frac{1}{2}$ of an 8-ounce can of dog food.

    a. Write an expression that can be use to determine how many ounces of dog food Jeff fed the dog on Wednesday.

    b. Write an expression that can be use to determine how many ounces of dog food Melody fed the dog on Friday.

    c. Who gave the dog more food, Jeff or Melody? Explain your answer.

4. For each statement 4a through 4d, circle YES if the statement is true or NO if the statement is not true.

    a. $\frac{5}{2} \times 3 > 3$ YES   NO

    b. $\frac{5}{2} \times 3 < \frac{5}{2}$ YES   NO

    c. $10 \times \frac{4}{5} < 10$ YES   NO

    d. $10 \times \frac{4}{5} > \frac{4}{5}$ YES   NO

5. For each pair of expressions, circle the greater product without finding the product.

    a. $\frac{3}{4} \times \frac{2}{3}$ and $\frac{3}{4} \times \frac{1}{2}$

    b. $\frac{2}{3} \times 3\frac{1}{4}$ and $\frac{4}{3} \times 3\frac{1}{4}$

    c. $\frac{3}{8} \times \frac{3}{8}$ and $\frac{3}{8} \times \frac{1}{2}$

Name _____

Common Core Standards Practice

5.NF.B.5b Interpret multiplication as scaling (resizing) by: Explaining why multiplying a given number by a fraction greater than 1 results in a product greater than the given number (recognizing multiplication by whole numbers greater than 1 as a familiar case); explaining why multiplying a given number by a fraction less than 1 results in a product smaller than the given number; and relating the principle of fraction equivalence $\frac{a}{b} = \frac{(n \times a)}{(n \times b)}$ to the effect of multiplying $\frac{a}{b}$ by 1.

1. Sam buys two carpets. One carpet is 3 feet by $\frac{7}{8}$ foot. The other carpet is 3 feet by $\frac{3}{4}$ foot.

   a. Which carpet has the greater area? Explain how you can find the answer without calculating either area.

   b. Which carpet has an area less than 3 square feet? How do you know?

2. Jasmine tapes together 3 straws in a straight line. Each straw is $9\frac{1}{2}$ inches long. To find the total length of the straws, Jasmine multiplies $9\frac{1}{2}$ by $\frac{3}{3}$.

   a. Describe the error Jasmine made.

   b. What is the value of the product that Jasmine found? Explain.

3. Explain why the product of 9 and $\frac{2}{3}$ is less than 9.

CC 35

4. The model shows three equal mixed numbers.

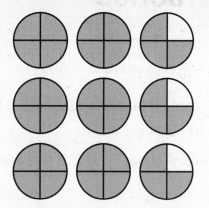

a. Write the product that the model represents.

b. How does the model show that the product is greater than 8?

5. Explain why the product of 12 and $\frac{3}{2}$ is greater than 12.

6. The equation shows two equivalent fractions.

$$\frac{8 \times ?}{10 \times ?} = \frac{48}{60}$$

a. What is the value of the question mark in the equation?

b. How do you know that $\frac{8}{10}$ and $\frac{48}{60}$ are equivalent?

c. Write another fraction that is equal to $\frac{8}{10}$.

Name _____

Common Core Standards Practice

5.NF.B.6 Solve real world problems involving multiplication of fractions and mixed numbers, e.g., by using visual fraction models or equations to represent the problem.

1. Mato's marinara recipe calls for $\frac{3}{4}$ tablespoon of tomato paste. He plans to make 12 batches of marinara. How much tomato paste will Mato need?

   a. Draw a model to represent the problem situation. Then find the solution.

2. John is training for a bicycle race. This week he rode his bicycle a total of 13 miles. Next week he plans to ride $2\frac{1}{2}$ times as far. How many miles will John ride his bicycle next week? Write an equation to represent the problem situation. Then solve the equation.

3. It snowed $37\frac{3}{4}$ inches last winter, which was 2 times more snow than the average. What is the average snow fall?

    a. Write an equation that matches the problem situation. Then solve the equation.

4. Alan's cake recipe requires $3\frac{2}{3}$ cups of flour. Alan is making 6 cakes. How much flour does he need?

    a. Draw a model to represent the problem situation.

    b. Write an equation to match the model you drew. Then solve the equation.

5. Julia and Awan are making a retangular banner. The banner will be $4\frac{1}{4}$ feet by $2\frac{3}{4}$ feet. What will be the area of the banner?

 CC 38

Name _____

Common Core Standards Practice

5.NF.B.7a Apply and extend previous understandings of division to divide unit fractions by whole numbers and whole numbers by unit fractions. Interpret division of a unit fraction by a non-zero whole number, and compute such quotients.

1. Five friends will share equally $\frac{1}{2}$ yard of felt for an art project. How much felt will each friend get?

   a. Use the model to represent the problem situation.

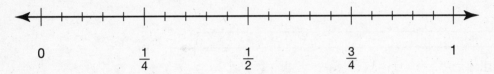

   b. Describe in words what the model shows.

   c. Write and solve an equation that matches the model.

2. A farmer will divide a $\frac{1}{4}$-acre plot of land into three equal-sized sections. What will be the size of each section?

   a. Use the model to represent the problem situation.

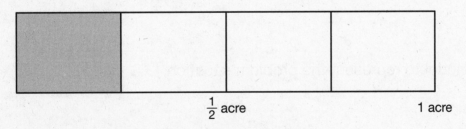

   b. Describe in words what the model shows.

   c. Write and solve an equation that matches the model.

3. Which of these models show $\frac{1}{5} \div 6$? Circle all that apply.

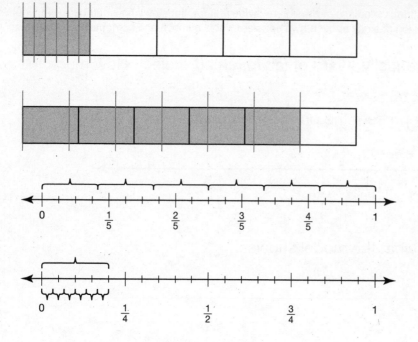

4. a. Describe a problem situation to match the equation below.

$$\frac{1}{3} \div 7 = \boxed{}$$

b. Draw a model to represent the problem situation.

c. Write and solve an equation that matches the model.

Name _____

Common Core Standards Practice

5.NF.B.7b Apply and extend previous understandings of division to divide unit fractions by whole numbers and whole numbers by unit fractions. Interpret division of a whole number by a unit fraction, and compute such quotients.

1. How many $\frac{1}{2}$-pound pieces are in a 3-pound piece of cheese?

   a. Complete the model to represent the problem situation.

                1 lb   2 lb   3 lb

   b. Describe in words what the model shows.

   c. Write and solve an equation to match the model.

2. How many $\frac{1}{4}$-mile segments are in a 2-mile relay?

   a. Complete the model to represent the problem situation.

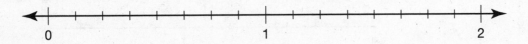

     0   1   2

   b. Describe in words what the model shows.

   c. Write and solve an equation that matches the model.

CC 41

3. a. Describe a problem situation that matches this model.

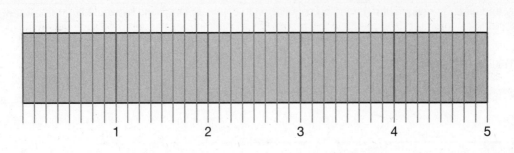

b. Write and solve an equation to match the model.

4. Match the model to the expression. Not all expressions match a model. Not all models match an expression.

$4 \div \frac{1}{4}$

$2 \div \frac{1}{6}$

$6 \div \frac{1}{3}$

$5 \div \frac{1}{2}$

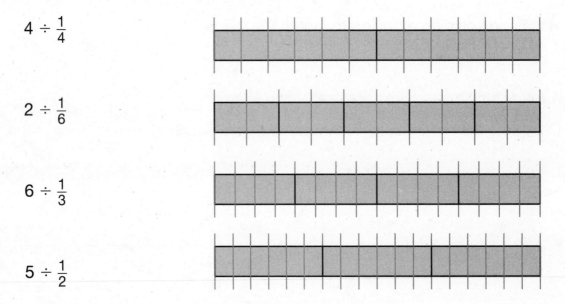

Name _____

Common Core Standards Practice

5.NF.B.7c Apply and extend previous understandings of division to divide unit fractions by whole numbers and whole numbers by unit fractions. Solve real world problems involving division of unit fractions by non-zero whole numbers and division of whole numbers by unit fractions, e.g., by using visual fraction models and equations to represent the problem.

1. Jimmy buys 3 whole pizzas. Each slice is $\frac{1}{8}$ of a pizza. How many slices are in all 3 pizzas?

   A 24

   B $\frac{1}{24}$

   C 32

   D $\frac{1}{32}$

2. Jack buys a bag of 5 apples, each equal in size. He eats $\frac{1}{2}$ of one apple. What fraction of the bag of apples did he eat?

   A 5

   B $\frac{1}{10}$

   C $\frac{1}{2}$

   D $\frac{2}{5}$

3. Jonny uses $\frac{1}{5}$ of a jar of dressing on 4 servings of salad. He uses an equal amount of dressing on each serving.

   a. Write an equation that can be used to determine the fraction of the jar of dressing that he uses on each serving.

   b. Solve the equation you wrote.

4. Debbi spent a total of 6 hours decorating her classroom. She worked in sessions that each lasted $\frac{1}{3}$ hour.

   a. Write an equation that can be used to determine how many sessions Debbi needed.

   b. Solve the equation you wrote.

5. Barry buys a plot of land that measures $\frac{1}{2}$ acre. He divides the plot into 5 equal pieces.

    a. Draw a model to illustrate the problem.

    b. What fraction of an acre is each piece?

6. A turtle walks at an average speed of $\frac{1}{3}$ mile per hour.

    a. Write an equation that can be used to find how long it would take the turtle to walk 2 miles.

    b. Solve the equation you wrote.

7. Mr. Smith has 7 cups of raisins. He likes to add $\frac{1}{4}$ cup of raisins to a bowl of cereal.

    a. Write an equation that can be used to determine how many bowls of cereal Mr. Smith can supply with raisins.

    b. Solve the equation you wrote.

8. a. Draw a model to illustrate the division problem $\frac{1}{5} \div 3$.

    b. Find the quotient.

CC 44

Name _____

Common Core Standards Practice

5.MD.A.1 Convert among different-sized standard measurement units within a given measurement system (e.g., convert 5 cm to 0.05 m), and use these conversions in solving multi-step, real world problems.

1. How many kilometers equal 1,200 meters?

   A 0.12

   B 1.2

   C 12

   D 120

2. How many pints are in 5.5 gallons?

   A 22

   B 33

   C 44

   D 55

3. Polly measures the height of a bookcase to be 2 feet, 10 inches.

   a. What is the height of the bookcase in inches?

   b. Is the height of the bookcase less than, equal to, or greater than 1 yard? Explain how you know.

4. Carl ran 120 feet, while his friend Eva ran 25 yards.

   a. Express 25 yards in feet.

   b. Express 120 feet in yards.

5. Which measurements are equal to 12 feet? Circle all that apply.

60 inches   4 yards   108 inches   3 yards

2 yards   120 inches   6 yards   144 inches

6. Which measurements are equal to 66 meters? Circle all that apply.

330 cm   3,300 cm   33,000 mm   0.33 km

0.66 km   6,600 cm   660 cm   66,000 mm

7. Jan's puppy has a mass of 3.9 kg. Alice's puppy has a mass of 2,750 g.

a. Write the mass of Alice's puppy in kilograms.

b. Whose puppy has a greater mass? Explain how you know.

8. Mike buys 4.5 meters of ribbon for a party.

a. What is the length of the ribbon in centimeters?

b. What is the length of the ribbon in millimeters?

Name _____

Common Core Standards Practice

5.MD.B.2 Make a line plot to display a data set of measurements in fractions of a unit ($\frac{1}{2}$, $\frac{1}{4}$, $\frac{1}{8}$). Use operations on fractions for this grade to solve problems involving information presented in line plots.

A teacher asked students to write the total number of hours that they each spent studying math and doing math homework in the last week. She recorded the data in a table.

Hours Spent on Math Last Week

$1\frac{1}{2}$	$1\frac{3}{4}$	$1\frac{1}{4}$	$2\frac{1}{4}$	$3\frac{1}{4}$	$\frac{3}{4}$	$2\frac{1}{2}$	$3\frac{3}{4}$	$5\frac{1}{4}$	$3\frac{1}{2}$	$4\frac{1}{4}$	$2\frac{1}{4}$
$3\frac{1}{2}$	$2\frac{3}{4}$	$2\frac{1}{2}$	$4\frac{3}{4}$	$3\frac{1}{2}$	$2\frac{1}{4}$	$3\frac{1}{4}$	$2\frac{3}{4}$	$2\frac{1}{4}$	$1\frac{3}{4}$	$3\frac{3}{4}$	$3\frac{1}{2}$

1. Make a line plot of this data.

2. How much longer was the greatest amount of time spent than the least amount of time spent on math last week?

3. How many times greater was the greatest amount of time spent than the least amount of time spent on math last week?

4. What were the two most common number of hours spent on math last week? What is the difference between those times?

CC 47

The students in two fifth grade classes recorded the number of miles they walked for the charity walk.

Miles Walked

2	$1\frac{3}{4}$	$2\frac{3}{4}$	$2\frac{1}{4}$	3	$3\frac{1}{4}$	$3\frac{1}{2}$	$3\frac{3}{4}$	4	$4\frac{1}{4}$	$4\frac{1}{2}$	$2\frac{1}{4}$
$6\frac{1}{2}$	$6\frac{1}{4}$	$3\frac{1}{2}$	4	$4\frac{1}{2}$	$4\frac{1}{4}$	$5\frac{1}{2}$	$4\frac{1}{4}$	6	3	$3\frac{3}{4}$	4
$4\frac{1}{4}$	$5\frac{1}{2}$	5	4	$3\frac{1}{2}$	$4\frac{1}{4}$	6	8	$5\frac{3}{4}$	$7\frac{1}{2}$	$5\frac{1}{2}$	$7\frac{1}{4}$

5. Make a line plot of the data.

6. What was the greatest difference between the number of miles walked by any two students?

7. Of the group of students who each walked $4\frac{1}{4}$ miles, how many miles did they walk in all?

8. Lisa and Jorge walked the second and third most miles. How many miles did Lisa and Jorge walk combined?

Name _____

Common Core Standards Practice

5.MD.C.3ab Recognize volume as an attribute of solid figures and understand concepts of volume measurement. A cube with side length 1 unit, called a "unit cube," is said to have "one cubic unit" of volume, and can be used to measure volume. A solid figure which can be packed without gaps or overlaps using *n* unit cubes is said to have a volume of *n* cubic units.

1. Which of these describes a measure of volume? Circle all that apply.

    the height of a wall   the number of tiles that cover a floor

    the distance around a yard   the number of packing peanuts in a box

    the amount of crushed rock   the amount of yard a garden takes up
    that fills a hole

2. Janelle has a large supply of small cubes, each the same size. How could she use the cubes to measure the volume of a shoebox?

3. Bill arranges 50 small cubes in a 5-by-10 array along a bookshelf. He claims that the volume of books that the shelf can hold is equal to 50 cubic units. Is his claim correct? If not, explain how he could find the volume.

4. Gill creates a model prism using 22 unit cubes. What is the volume of the prism?

    A 11 units

    B 22 units

    C 22 cubic units

    D 66 cubic units

5. A box has a volume of 64 cubic units. How many cubes with a volume of 1 cubic unit can fit in the box?

    A 4

    B 8

    C 16

    D 64

6. Walter's father put mulch around some trees in the yard. Walter measured the depth of the mulch. He found that there was 2 inches of mulch around each tree. Does the measurement of 2 inches show exactly how much mulch Walter's father used around each tree? Explain why or why not.

7. A closet measures 5 feet wide and 3 feet deep. Does the measurement of 15 square feet show the volume inside the closet? If not, how could you find the volume inside the closet?

Common Core Standards Practice

5.MD.C.4 Measure volumes by counting unit cubes, using cubic cm, cubic in, cubic ft, and improvised units.

Count the cubes to determine the volume of each shape. There are no hidden cubes.

1.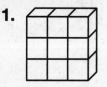

  A 10 cubic units
  B 9 cubic units
  C 12 cubic units
  D 5 cubic units

2.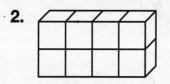

  A 10 cubic units
  B 5 cubic units
  C 8 cubic units
  D 5 cubic units

3.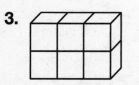

  A 6 cubic units
  B 8 cubic units
  C 12 cubic units
  D 15 cubic units

4.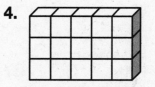

  A 6 cubic units
  B 9 cubic units
  C 10 cubic units
  D 15 cubic units

In these shapes, the volume of each cube is 1 cubic centimeters. Find the volume of each shape in cubic centimeters.

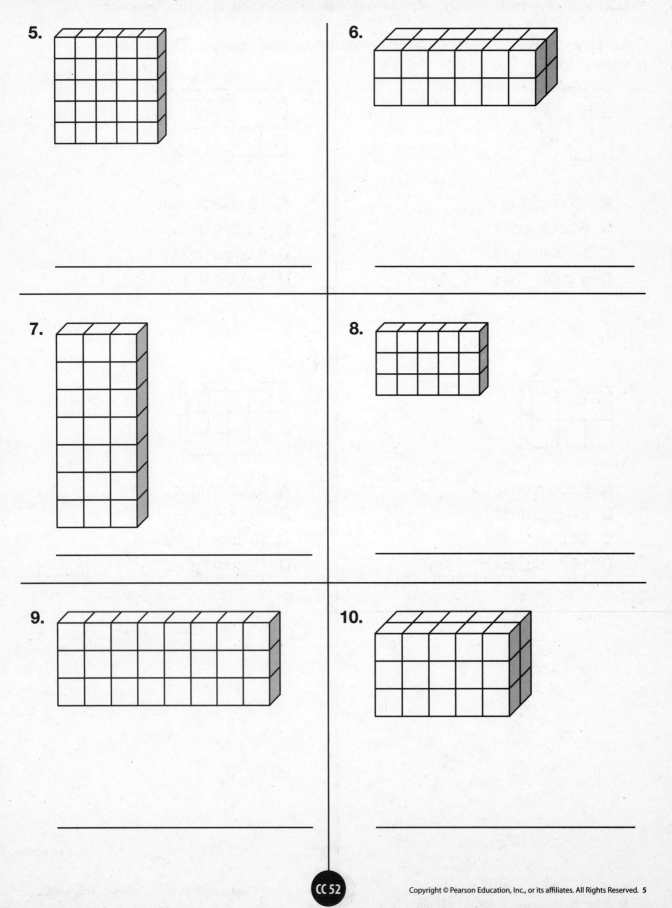

5. _____

6. _____

7. _____

8. _____

9. _____

10. _____

Name _____

Common Core Standards Practice

5.MD.C.5a Relate volume to the operations of multiplication and addition and solve real world and mathematical problems involving volume. Find the volume of a right rectangular prism with whole-number side lengths by packing it with unit cubes, and show that the volume is the same as would be found by multiplying the edge lengths, equivalently by multiplying the height by the area of the base. Represent threefold whole-number products as volumes, e.g., to represent the associative property of multiplication.

Find the volumes of the rectangular prisms shown below.

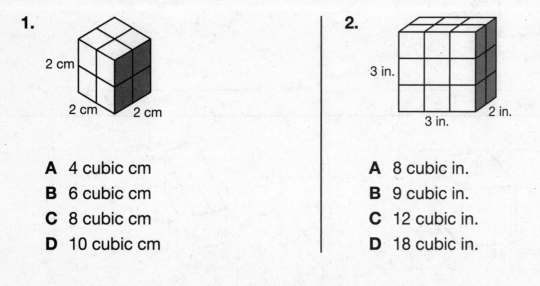

1.

2 cm
2 cm 2 cm

A 4 cubic cm
B 6 cubic cm
C 8 cubic cm
D 10 cubic cm

2.

3 in.
3 in. 2 in.

A 8 cubic in.
B 9 cubic in.
C 12 cubic in.
D 18 cubic in.

3. Tell two ways to find the volume of the box shown below.

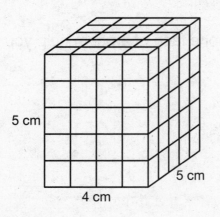

5 cm
5 cm
4 cm

One way

Another way

4. Find the volume for each of these rectangular prisms.

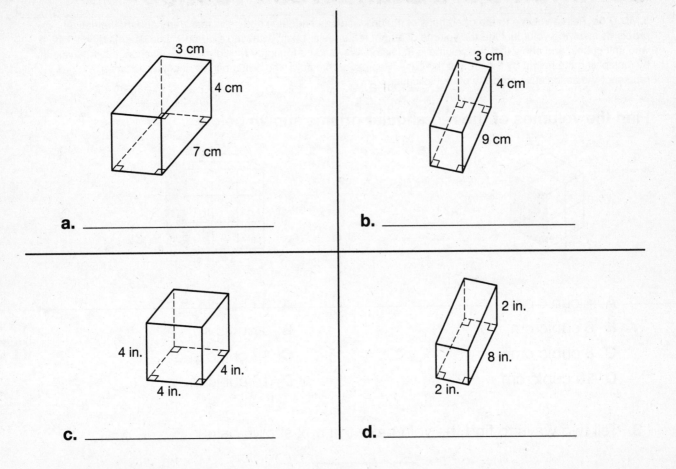

a. _____

b. _____

c. _____

d. _____

5. How does knowing the area of one face of a prism help you find the volume of the prism?

Name _____

Common Core Standards Practice

5.MD.C.5b Relate volume to the operations of multiplication and addition and solve real world and mathematical problems involving volume. Apply the formulas $V = l \times w \times h$ and $V = b \times h$ for rectangular prisms to find volumes of right rectangular prisms with whole-number edge lengths in the context of solving real world and mathematical problems.

1. A milk carton is in the shape of a rectangular prism that is 6 inches long, 4 inches wide, and 4 inches tall. What is its volume?

2. A room is in the shape of a rectangular prism that is 13 feet long, 10 feet high, and 11 feet wide. What is its volume?

3. A bank vault is in the shape of a rectangular prism with a floor area of 280 square feet and a height of 19 feet. Calculate its volume.

4. Calculate the volume of the jewelry box shown below.

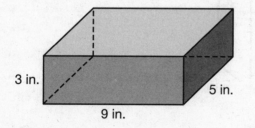

3 in.   5 in.   9 in.

5. A dumpster is in the shape of a rectangular prism. Its base measures 136 square feet, and its height is 6 feet. What is the volume of the dumpster?

6. The antique bottle shown below consists of a rectangular prism and a cylinder-shaped spout. Find the volume of the prism section of the bottle.

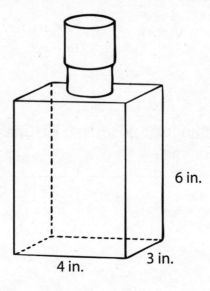

6 in.

3 in.

4 in.

7. Kyle will fill the candle mold shown below with liquid wax. Find the amount of liquid wax that the mold can hold.

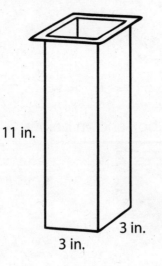

11 in.

3 in.

3 in.

8. Victor keeps a rabbit in a cage that has the shape of a rectangular prism. The ends of the cage measures 4 square feet and the cage is 3 feet long. What is the volume of the cage?

Name _____

Common Core Standards Practice

5.MD.C.5c Relate volume to the operations of multiplication and addition and solve real world and mathematical problems involving volume. Recognize volume as additive. Find volumes of solid figures composed of two non-overlapping right rectangular prisms by adding the volumes of the non-overlapping parts, applying this technique to solve real world problems.

Find the volume of each individual prism. Then add the volumes to find the volume of the combined prisms.

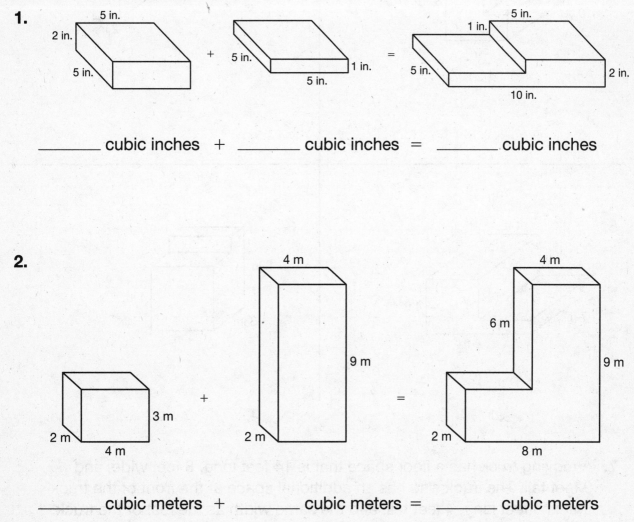

1.

_____ cubic inches + _____ cubic inches = _____ cubic inches

2.

_____ cubic meters + _____ cubic meters = _____ cubic meters

Find the volume of these shapes. Each was made by joining two rectangular prisms together.

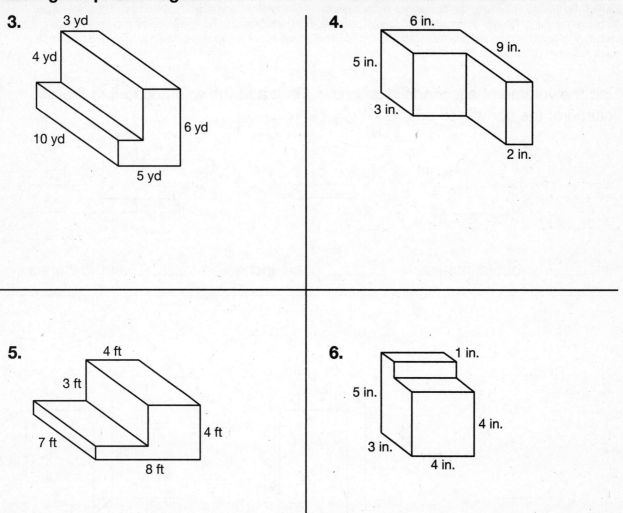

3. 3 yd
4 yd
10 yd
5 yd
6 yd

4. 6 in.
9 in.
5 in.
3 in.
2 in.

5. 4 ft
3 ft
7 ft
8 ft
4 ft

6. 1 in.
5 in.
4 in.
3 in.
4 in.

7. A moving truck has a floor space that is 14 feet long, 8 feet wide, and 9 feet tall. The truck also has an additional space at the front of the truck that is 3 feet long, 4 feet tall, and the same width as the rest of the truck. How much space is there inside the moving truck?

CC 58

Name _____

Common Core Standards Practice

5.G.A.1 Use a pair of perpendicular number lines, called axes, to define a coordinate system, with the intersection of the lines (the origin) arranged to coincide with the 0 on each line and a given point in the plane located by using an ordered pair of numbers, called its coordinates. Understand that the first number indicates how far to travel from the origin in the direction of one axis, and the second number indicates how far to travel in the direction of the second axis, with the convention that the names of the two axes and the coordinates correspond (e.g., x-axis and x-coordinate, y-axis and y-coordinate).

Use the coordinate plane below for Exercises 1–3.

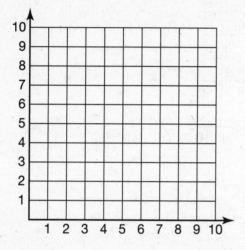

1. Label these parts of the coordinate plane.

    a. x-axis

    b. y-axis

    c. O

2. Draw and label a line to show where the x-coordinate is always equal to 6.

3. Draw and label a line to show where the y-coordinate is always equal to 3.

Use the coordinate plane below to find the point that matches each description. Name each point with a letter and its coordinates.

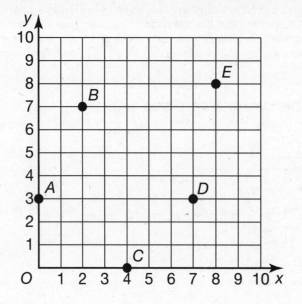

4. the point on the *x*-axis _____

5. the point on the *y*-axis _____

6. the point that has an *x*-coordinate of 7 _____

7. the point that has a *y*-coordinate of 7 _____

8. the point that has *x*- and *y*-coordinates that equal each other _____

Common Core Standards Practice

5.G.A.2 Represent real world and mathematical problems by graphing points in the first quadrant of the coordinate plane, and interpret coordinate values of points in the context of the situation.

1. Write the coordinates for the points shown in the coordinate plane.

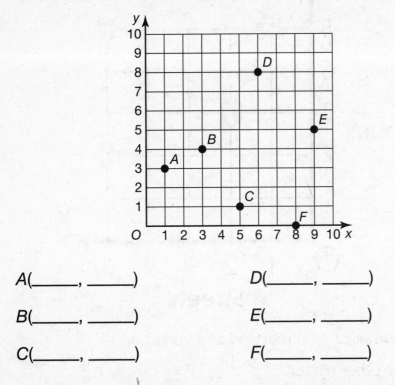

A(_____ , _____)   D(_____ , _____)

B(_____ , _____)   E(_____ , _____)

C(_____ , _____)   F(_____ , _____)

2. Graph and label these points in the coordinate plane.

A(3, 4)   D(8, 9)

B(5, 5)   E(2, 8)

C(7, 2)   F(0, 5)

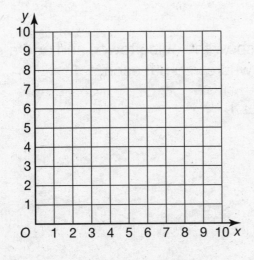

3. Downtown has streets and avenues that fit the coordinate plane, as shown in the map below.

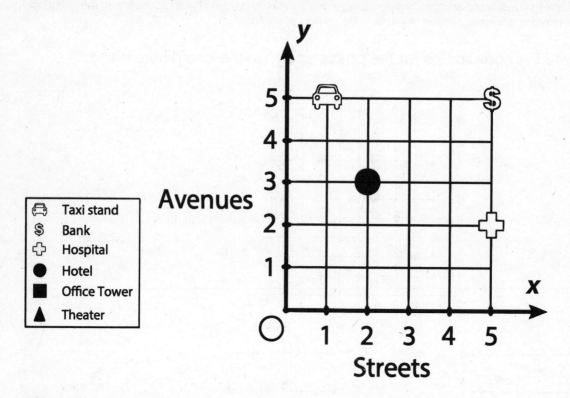

The taxi stand is at the corner of 1st Street and 5th Avenue.

Name the locations of the other places.

a. Hotel:

b. Bank:

c. Hospital:

4. Add a square to the map to show the office tower, and add a triangle to show the theater. Identify where you put each.

a. Office tower: (_____, _____)

b. Theater: (_____, _____)

Name _____

Common Core Standards Practice

5.G.B.3 Understand that attributes belonging to a category of two-dimensional figures also belong to all subcategories of that category.

1. What properties do isosceles and equilateral triangles share?

2. What properties do rhombuses and parallelograms share?

3. Here are a rectangle, a square, and a rhombus.

 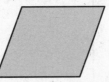

    a. What are the common properties of the rectangle and the square?

    b. What are the common properties of the square and the rhombus?

    c. Of the three figures, which could also be classified as either of the other two figures? Explain.

 CC 63

4. Name a common property of trapezoids and quadrilaterals.

5. Put check marks in the table to show each figure that has the given property.

Property	Quadrilateral	Parallelogram	Trapezoid	Rectangle	Rhombus	Square
This figure has four sides.						
This figure always has two pairs of parallel sides.						
This figure has only one pair of parallel sides.						
This figure always has four right angles.						
This figure always has four sides of equal length.						

Name _____

Common Core Standards Practice

5.G.B.4 Classify two-dimensional figures in a hierarchy based on properties.

1. A triangle has one right angle. Two of its sides are equal in length. Which terms describe the triangle? Circle all that apply.

   right   isosceles   scalene   equilateral

Use the chart below to help you classify quadrilaterals.

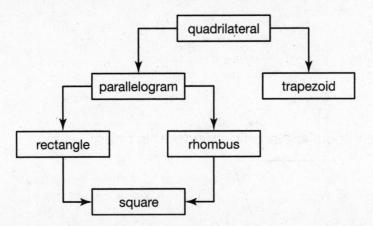

2. A figure has four sides and four right angles. The lengths of its sides are not all equal to each other. Which names could describe the figure? Circle all that apply.

   quadrilateral   trapezoid   parallelogram   rhombus   rectangle   square

3. Name the figure in as many ways as possible.

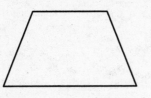

   A quadrilateral
   B quadrilateral, parallelogram
   C quadrilateral, trapezoid
   D quadrilateral, parallelogram, rhombus

4. Name this figure.

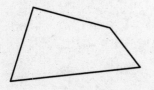

5. Name this figure in as many ways as possible.

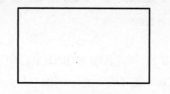

6. Select the most specific classification for a figure that has four sides of equal length, but not four angles of equal measure.

   A quadrilateral

   B parallelogram

   C rhombus

   D trapezoid

7. What is the most specific classification for this figure?

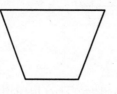

   A quadrilateral   **C** trapezoid

   B parallelogram   **D** rhombus

8. Why are all rectangles examples of parallelograms, but all parallelograms are not rectangles?

9. Circle the statements that are true.

All squares are rectangles.

All rhombuses are squares.

All quadrilaterals are trapezoids.

All rhombuses are parallelograms.

All parellograms are quadrilaterals.

Name _____

Practice End-of-Year Assessment

1. Tell two ways you can use to find the volume of a rectangular prism.

One Way	**Another Way**

2. A triangle has three sides of equal length. Circle the categories in which the triangle can be classified.

equilateral   isosceles   right   scalene

3. A rectangular rug is $5\frac{3}{4}$ feet wide and $7\frac{1}{2}$ feet long. What is the area of the rug?

4. To make a lace border for a hat, Rebecca uses $\frac{5}{12}$ yard of red lace and $\frac{1}{6}$ yard of green lace.

   a. Model the problem with this circle.

   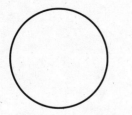

   b. How much lace does Rebecca use to make her hat?

5. Cassie's cat weighs $3\frac{1}{2}$ pounds. Her dog weighs 4 times as much as her cat. How much does her dog weigh?

6. Which describes the relationship between 15,700 and 157,000?

   A 15,700 is $\frac{1}{10}$ of 157,000.

   B 157,000 is $\frac{1}{10}$ of 15,700.

   C 15,700 is $\frac{1}{100}$ of 157,000.

   D 157,000 is $\frac{1}{100}$ of 15,700.

7. Find the quotient.

   1,633 ÷ 23.

8. The line plot shows the birth weights, in pounds, of a litter of 8 puppies.

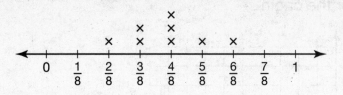

a. What is the difference in weight between the heaviest and lightest puppy?

b. Which birth weight was most common among the puppies?

9. How is the value of 3 in the number 43,442 different from the value of 3 in the number 44,432?

10. Which model matches the division expression?

$3 \div 4$

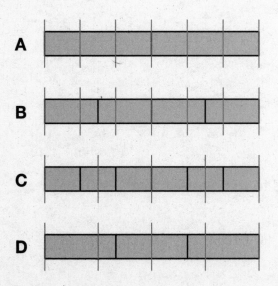

11. Label the *x*-axis, *y*-axis, and origin on the coordinate grid shown below. Use the letter "O" for the origin.

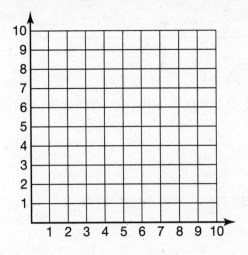

12. Match these numbers with their expanded forms.

7.5 $\qquad$ $7 \times 1 + 0 \times \frac{1}{10} + 5 \times \frac{1}{100}$

7.05 $\qquad$ $1 \times 1000 + 6 \times 100 + 8 \times 1$

16.09 $\qquad$ $1 \times 10 + 6 \times 1 + 9 \times \frac{1}{100}$

1,608 $\qquad$ $7 \times 1 + 5 \times \frac{1}{10}$

13. Divide.

0.84 ÷ 0.07

14. Which of these numbers, when rounded to the nearest tenth, is 0.8? Circle all that round to 0.8.

0.76 $\qquad$ 0.84 $\qquad$ 0.72 $\qquad$ 0.079 $\qquad$ 0.79

15. Look at the following pairs of values.

x	y
1	5
2	8
3	11
4	14
5	17

a. What is the rule for each column?

b. Write two more pairs of values that could be added to this table.

c. Graph these pairs of values on the coordinate grid. What do you notice about the graph of these values?

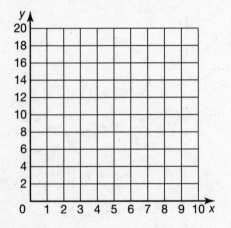

16. Dao has a cookie recipe that calls for $3\frac{1}{4}$ cups of flour. He plans to make $1\frac{1}{2}$ batches of cookies. Explain whether Dao will need more flour, less flour, or the same amount of flour as his recipe calls for.

17. Write the expressions in the appropriate place. You should NOT find the products of the expressions.

Less than 3	Equal to 3	Greater than 3

$$\frac{1}{3} \times 3 \qquad\qquad \frac{6}{6} \times 3 \qquad\qquad \frac{7}{6} \times 3 \qquad\qquad 3 \times \frac{7}{7}$$

$$3 \times \frac{3}{2} \qquad\qquad 3 \times \frac{2}{5} \qquad\qquad 3 \times \frac{9}{7} \qquad\qquad \frac{1}{4} \times 6$$

18. Tell whether the equation is true. Justify your answer.

$$36 - (12 + 8) \div 4 \overset{?}{=} 36 - 12 + 8 \div 4$$

19. Complete the table.

32.8 ÷ 1	32.8
32.8 ÷ 10	
32.8 ÷ 100	
32.8 ÷ 1,000	

Describe the pattern in the table.

20. The length of a rectangular window is $5\frac{3}{4}$ feet and its width is $3\frac{1}{2}$ feet. What is the area of the window?

21. Plot points *M* and *L* on the coordinate grid.

    a. Point *M*: (7, 3)

    b. Point *L*: (3, 1)

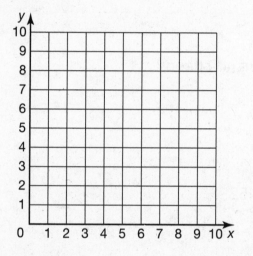

22. Paula covers her bathroom with pink and white tiles. Each tile is the same size. She uses $2\frac{1}{2}$ times more pink tiles than white tiles, and the white tiles cover $4\frac{1}{2}$ square feet. How much area do the pink tiles cover?

23. A concert hall has 2,312 seats. For one concert, each seat is sold for $89. What is the total amount of money in ticket sales if the concert is sold out?

24. A recipe calls for $\frac{2}{3}$ cup of brown sugar to make one batch of muffins. Amanda plans to make $5\frac{1}{2}$ batches of muffins.

    a. Draw a model to match the problem situation.

    b. How much brown sugar will Amanda need?

25. Find the product of 1,275 and 23,452.

26. Which of these are equal to the sum of $\frac{4}{12}$ and $\frac{6}{8}$? Circle all that are equal to the sum.

$\frac{10}{20}$ $\frac{26}{24}$ $\frac{10}{12}$ $\frac{13}{12}$ $1\frac{1}{12}$ $1\frac{2}{12}$

27. Mary studied math for $1\frac{1}{2}$ hours and science for $\frac{3}{5}$ hour. How many hours did she spend studying?

28. Which expression matches this statement?
four times the difference of 12 and 2

    A $4 + 12 - 2$

    B $12 - 2 \times 4$

    C $4 \times (12 - 2)$

    D $4 \times 12 - 2$

29. A dolphin ate 2,604 pounds of fish during the 31 days of March.

    a. What is the average amount of fish the dolphin ate per day?

    b. Draw a model to justify your answer.

30. Pineapples cost $2.19 each. Watermelons cost $2.91 each.

    a. Which costs more: a pineapple or a watermelon?

    b. Write a number sentence to compare the two prices.

CC 75

31. A group of 6 friends wants to share 8 pears evenly. All of the pears are the same size.

    a. How many pears should each friend receive?

    b. Explain how the friends should cut the pears and divide them.

32. Drake has a piece of blue ribbon that is $\frac{1}{8}$ yard long, and a silver ribbon that is $\frac{3}{4}$ yard long. How much longer is the silver ribbon?

33. Amy has 6 cups of applesauce. She divides the applesauce into $\frac{1}{2}$-cup servings.

    a. Draw a model to match the problem.

    b. How many servings of applesauce does she have?

34. A sporting goods factory produces 13,234 tennis balls per month. How many tennis balls does it produce during 12 months?

35. Emilio builds a flower planter in the shape of a rectangular prism. It is 4 feet long, 2 feet high, and 2 feet wide. What is the volume of the planter?

36. Four friends share $\frac{1}{4}$ of a cake. What fraction of the whole cake does each friend get?

37. Which term could describe each of these three figures?

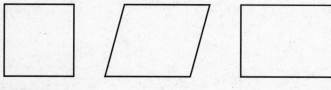

A square
B rhombus
C rectangle
D parallelogram

38. Which of these are equal to the difference of $\frac{4}{6}$ and $\frac{2}{9}$? Circle all that are equal to the difference.

$\frac{1}{9}$ $\qquad$ $\frac{4}{9}$ $\qquad$ $\frac{2}{3}$ $\qquad$ $\frac{8}{18}$ $\qquad$ $\frac{3}{6}$ $\qquad$ $\frac{8}{9}$

39. Find the volume of the rectangular prism shown below.

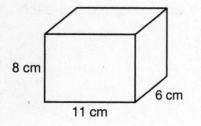

8 cm

11 cm

6 cm

40. Multiply.

9.3×4.27

41. Draw a model to find the product of $\frac{3}{8} \times 4$. Then find the product.

42. What is 17.264 rounded to the nearest hundredth?

    A 17.26

    B 17.27

    C 17.3

    D 17.24

43. Bargain Toys packs 1,440 toys onto 40 shelves. Each shelf holds the same number of toys. How many toys are on each shelf?

44. Circle all of the expressions that equal 1,483,000.

    1.483×10^6 14.83×10^6 148.3×10^4

    148.3×10^3 1.483×10^7 14.83×10^5

45. Mr. Lee's fence is 10 yards long. How many feet long is the fence?

Name _____

Performance Task 1

Storage Needs

Part A

Erica makes and sells homemade salad dressings. She packages the dressings in small jars, which she then places in boxes that hold 6 jars. The dimensions of the shipping boxes are 1 foot by 1 foot by 1 foot.

Erica has two different storage spaces for the boxes. One of the spaces is 4 feet long by 3 wide feet by 6 feet high. The other space measures 5 feet long by 3 feet wide by 5 feet high.

1. Into which storage area can Erica fit more boxes of dressing? How many more boxes can she fit into the larger area? Explain your answer with models.

Part B

Erica would like to increase the production of her salad dressings. To do so, she will need more storage space for boxes of jars. Erica has two options for additional storage space. Storage space C is 4 feet long by 6 feet wide by 6 feet high and storage space D is 8 feet long by 4 feet wide by 5 feet high. Including her original storage area, Erica would like to have a total of at least 280 cubic feet, but no more than 300 cubic feet, of storage space.

2. Which of the two additional storage space options should Erica choose? Explain your reasoning for the option you selected.

Name _____

Performance Task 2

Town Beautification

Part A

The Town Council in Center City will start a tree-planting program to beautify parts of the town. The plan calls for planting 2,000 trees. Below are three types of trees that have been recommended and are available for planting:

Type of Tree	Cost per Tree (including tax)
Cherry	$40.50
Dogwood	$65.00
Myrtle	$50.50

The Town Council voted to budget $100,000 to buy the 2,000 trees. Both the Parks Department, which will purchase and plant the trees, and the Town Council, agree that there should be a mix of all three types of trees.

The towns people were also surveyed about which types of trees to plant. The result of the survey show that cherry trees are a town favorite, so the Town Council has recommended that at least half of the trees planted be cherry trees.

1. You have been asked by the Parks Department to determine how many of each type of tree the Parks Department should purchase and the total cost. In your proposal, you should come as close as you can to spending all of the money budgeted for the purchase of the trees. You need to answer these questions in your proposal:

   a. What is the total number of each type of tree to be planted?

   b. What is the total amount needed to purchase each type of tree?

   c. What is the total amount needed to purchase all types of trees?

Part B

The Parks Department will be responsible for planting all of the trees for the tree-planting program. According to the tree nursery, each newly planted tree will need a layer of organic mulch. The nursery estimates that each cherry tree planted will require 20 pounds of mulch, each dogwood tree 25 pounds of mulch, and each myrtle tree 20 pounds of mulch. The nursery sells mulch for $34.95 a ton. It does not sell fractions of a ton.

2. How much money will the Parks Department need in order to purchase mulch for all of the trees in your proposal?